FOCUSED FAITH

KEEPING YOUR FAITH IN GOD WHEN LIFE HAS GONE WRONG

Frankie Miller

Copyright © 2025 by Frankie Miller

Books Academy LLC

112 SW HK Dodgen Loop,
Temple, Texas 76504

Hotline: (254) 800-1189

Ordering Information: Quantity sales. Special discounts are available on quantity purchases by corporations, associations, and others. For details, contact the publisher at the address above.

Printed in the United States of America.

ISBN: Softcover: 978-1-968807-28-3

eBook: 978-1-968807-29-0

PREFACE

When I became a Christian on October 13, 1996, I had no idea how much God would change my life. I didn't grow up in church, you see. My parents would attend church once in a while or just watch ministry on the television. I grew up in Brooklyn, New York, born on June 6, 1971, born to Frank Miller Jr. and Mildred Miller. My parents provided a lot of love, but they weren't Christians, so I grew up knowing that there is a God but never knowing what it meant to be in relationship with him or that it was even possible to be in relationship with him.

Now that I know how much God gave to have a relationship with me, I'm forever grateful and know how undeserving I am of his grace. So, in this book, I am giving those that know the Lord Jesus Christ and those that may not, a snapshot of living a life of faith on a day-to-day basis. With God on your side, no matter what comes your way, you will always end up on top! Why, because Jesus Christ has overcome the world via his resurrection from the dead! Heh, haa... nuff said.

INTRODUCTION

Don't give up hope in Jesus Christ!
Proverbs chapter 3 verses 5-6 says, "Trust in the Lord with all your heart and lean not on your own understanding, in all your ways, acknowledge him and he shall direct your paths."

I never thought in my wildest dreams that God Almighty would call me to write books that will save the lives of the people that read them, heh, haa. I mean, after all, this is the only reason why I am writing books about my testimonies of what the Lord Jesus Christ has done for me—to introduce people to Jesus Christ as a God who loved them and who wants a real relationship with them. He is also a God who will be faithful to you, especially in your time of greatest need. You can count on Jesus Christ to walk with you through whatever may be going on in your life!

Furthermore, I would say that hope is found in the Holy Bible; there is no other book that will inspire you to press on in life despite of the obstacles that you may be facing than the word of God! As the Bible declares in 1 Peter chapter 2 verse 6, "Therefore it is also contained in the Scripture, 'Behold, I lay in Zion a chief cornerstone, elect, precious and he who believes on him, will by no means be put to shame." Basically, if you put your faith in Jesus Christ, ultimately you won't ever be put to shame. Jesus Christ is my hope in this life and the life to come. I truly hope that this book of my personal journeys in faith will inspire you to

CONTENTS

CHAPTER 1

FOCUSED FAITH:

Keeping Your Faith In God
When Life Has Gone Wrong

The biblical book of James declares in chapter 1 verses 2-8, "My brethren, count it all joy when you fall into various trials, knowing that the testing of your faith produces patience. But let patience have its perfect work, that you may be perfect and complete, lacking nothing. If any of you lacks wisdom, let him ask of God, who gives to all liberally and without reproach and it will be given to him. But let him ask in faith, with no doubting, for he who doubts is like a wave of the sea, driven and tossed by the wind. For let not that man suppose that he will receive anything from the Lord. He is a double-minded man, unstable in all his ways." low gig

A young man had been consistently living this scripture out on a daily basis ever since he gave his heart to serving the Lord Jesus Christ a.k.a. born-again Christian. He was saved spirit-filled believer in Jesus Christ! Along his journey with following Christ, there were various times where his *faith* is tested to the breaking point, like the time when he lost six jobs over a five-year span. You see, he was an aircraft mechanic by trade and he was married with a wife, no children though, but they had to two dogs, a mortgage, two car notes, two student loans, and everyday utilities to pay.

This young couple did give tithes and offerings faithfully to their local church that they are members of and attend regularly for they follow the biblical principles of stewardship, which is outlined in 2 Corinthians chapter 9 verse 6-9, "But this I say, he who sows sparingly, will also reap sparingly and he who sows bountifully, will also reap bountifully. So let each one give as he purposes in his heart, not grudgingly or of necessity, for God loves a cheerful giver. And God is able to make all Grace abound toward you, that you, always having sufficiency in all things, may have an abundance for every good work." So the young man began to question within himself if the biblical scriptures concerning giving really were true.

Although he and his wife gave to God *cheerfully*, both of them up to the point had seen no tangible evidence that what they were doing is helping them financially especially as the layoffs piled up every other year. So yes, their faith was being tested in their lives as to whether they "trust God or not!"

✶✶✶✶✶

Despite of the young couple's financial situation, they continue to sow into the kingdom of God via their local church. You see, you don't really know yourself if you trust God at all unless you have circumstances happening in your life that contradict the scriptures. If you still follow the scriptures in spite of your circumstances, then you have proven to yourself that you really trust God.

The truth is, people, many can say that they trust and believe in the Lord when things are going well, but how about when things are going wrong? Will you still trust God and obey his word?
The Bible declares in the book of Galatians chapter 5 verse 9, "And let us not grow weary, while doing good, for in due season, we shall reap, if we don't lose heart." The message that the Lord is saying to people is to now quit on anything, especially if God is on your side! He can change your circumstances. And if your circumstances don't change right away (which often times they don't), then he will change your perspective or how you view your problem, helping you to endure the hardship! This is what he did for the young couple, their financial situation gradually changed over time, but the Lord helped them to endure the hardship, in the meantime.

CHAPTER 2

When Things Don't Look Like They Should

It is important to note that the Bible declares in Romans chapter 8 verse 28, "And we know that all things work together for good, to these who love God to those who are the called according to his purpose." God knows your end before your beginning because he is God! So in light of that, the young man challenged himself; why not trust God then?

When things don't look like they should in your life, believe the Bible anyways, because God cannot lie!

This young couple had been in financial strains for years; even though they obeyed the Bible, obedience didn't exempt them from trouble. Some Christians believe (falsely) that if they obey all of the scriptures, that will keep them from suffering on any level in life When in fact the Bible declares in Acts chapter 9 verses 15-16, "But: the Lord said to him; Go for he (Apostle Paul) is a chosen vessel d mine to bear my name before Gentiles, Kings and the children of Israel. For I will show him how many things he must suffer for my name's sake."

This passage of scripture refers to Paul's conversion on the roid after his encounter with Jesus Christ. So clearly, suffering for Christ's sake, especially when obeying God's Word, should be expected y the believer. I mean, if you're a Christian who thinks that they won't have to suffer, then you need to get a better understanding of God's Word! Heh, haa... because suffering comes with the territory, people.

The young man (believer) who I refer to in this book has been experiencing everything that I just mentioned in his walk with the Lord Jesus Christ! As I first gave reference to his plight back in chapter 1, things certainly didn't look like they should for a season in his life. But slowly and surely, as he and his wife kept believing, by meditating on God's Word (Bible) and seeking God in Prayer on a daily basis, as well as attending their local church regularly, God began to turn their financial situation around.

Keep in mind, people, that if the Lord hasn't turned your situation around yet, it is because he is moved to act by seeing your faith in him over a period of time. While the Lord is concerned about your situation, he will only fix it when he sees sustained faith from the believer. Time is not an issue with God, whenever he comes through for you, it will always be just in time...heh, haa...so "trust him when you can't trace him" is the slogan that the seasoned believer proclaims!

CHAPTER 3

Staying Encouraged by the Word of God

One of the most valuable tools of the believer is the Word of God (Bible). The more that a believer in Christ will meditate in the Bible, the less power his or her situation will have over them. You see, the more that you meditate on the scriptures, the more your faith in God will increase, for the Bible declares in 2 Corinthians chapter 5 verse 7, "For we walk by faith, not by sight." In essence, God is saying to us that don't put your focus or attention on what your situation oi circumstances are showing you. But instead, fix your eyes upon what your *Heavenly Father* has already said about you.

When you walk by faith, it will always contradict your present situation, and it is important to remember this fact while we go through difficult situations. This is the reason why we as Christians need to know the scriptures in the Bible by memory. Because when we do, the Holy Spirit of God can bring to remembrance to us of what he has already declared through the *finished works* of Christ on the cross, what he has already said about us. So, no matter what you're going through, there is a passage or story in the Bible that will address your circumstance, and it will provide encouragement to you in your time of need. God cannot lie or change his mind about us though he loves us!

I would also add that if you're a *Christian* that is actively involved in the doing of the Great Commission that Christ gave of "Go ye into all the World and Preach the Gospel" via your local church (by getting involved by volunteering and giving of your resources) a.k.a. feeding the hungry and clothing the naked or just sharing your faith with someone who is doing worse off than yourself, that will automatically keep you encouraged because it will be a constant reminder of how *grateful* you should be to the Lord. Because compared to your situation, as bad as it may be, the person who you're ministering to has got it a lot worse. The Bible declares in Philippians chapter 4 verse 11, "Not that I speak in regard to need, for I have learned in whatever state I am, to be content."

*****

Being content is the way your attitude should be, no matter the situation. I'm not saying that it is easy to do, but that is where you ask the Lord to help you. You will find the Holy Spirit will enable you to have a grateful and content attitude, while your life burns like a California Forest Fire...heh, haa...I'm just kidding. But I am speaking from a place of experience while going through my various trials and tribulations over the years has taught me, that I don't have it as bad as someone else, especially when I begin to reach out of my own place of need and help others who are less *blessed* than me or my family. You will also find that as you get involved with helping others, God will begin to take care of your situation without you even having to ask or pray about it. So, develop an attitude of gratitude because God is good all the time!

This is why I feel church membership is so vitally important to the spiritual growth of a believer in Christ. When you are an active member, serving others in your local church out in your local community, following the *vision* established by your local church leadership, then you grow in your faith in God. A believer that is not involved in their local church will not grow spiritually, and unless they do join a local assembly of believers, they will never be challenged to walk out their faith, where they will eventually develop an attitude of gratitude out of the abundance of service to others. Once you develop an attitude of gratitude, your problems or circumstances, though serious, will become easier to walk through on a day-to-day basis.

CHAPTER 4

Making Prayer a Priority

Prayer should be your first response rather than your last resort, especially when life gives you a "kick in the head." Your time spent with God in prayer will carry you through anything that life will throw your way. The Bible declares in Isiah chapter 43 verses 1-2, "But now, thus says the Lord, who created you, O Jacob and he who formed you O Israel; fear not, for I have redeemed you. I have called you by name. You are mine. When you pass through the waters, I will be with you. And through the rivers, they shall not overthrow you.

When you walk through the fire, you shall not be burned, nor shall the flame scorch you!" Wow! How committed is God to us! Thank you, Lord!

When you get into the presence of the Lord, you can leave all your problems with him, there with Jesus, by the power of the Holy Spirit. Prayer is more caught than just taught; I learned to pray by just doing it as the Holy Spirit gave me the urge to come. I have a certain place in my home where I seek God on a daily basis. I personally seek God at least two times a day—morning time and evening time. I find the more that I seek the Lord, the better prepared I am to tackle the day and what it may bring my way.

Prayer is simply "talking to the Lord." It has nothing to do with being religious as some may say; prayer has everything to do with being relational with God, which is what Jesus died on the cross for us to have—a relationship through him with the Father in heaven.

So, as you practice praying, it will eventually become something that is just like a reflex to you. And over time, it will be something you of your time with the Lord. can't do without. The power of prayer is real, so take full advantage of your time with the Lord.

*****

As you pray, it builds your "faith in God as well." I can't begin to describe how many times that I've been at the end of my rope literally, and the Lord helped me cope and helped me get through the circumstance. The Bible declares in Luke chapter 18 verse 1, "Men ought always to pray and not lose heart." The Bible also declares in John chapter 15 verse 16, "You did not choose me, but I chose you and appointed you that you should go and bear fruit and that your fruit should remain, that whatever you ask the Father in my name he may give you." There is no other name that we can use to pray to the Father. Jesus Christ is the only name that the Father in heaven acknowledges. We do not go to the Father through a man, neither can we go to the Father directly.

Jesus Christ declared in John chapter 14 verse 6, "That I am the way, the truth and the light and no man comes to the Father except by me." So clearly your personal walk with God will only come through Jesus alone and by the power of his Holy Spirit. So being a born-again Christian, or saved as we would say, is sooo... very important when we are maintaining our faith in God; when things go wrong, God can turn them around in your favor! Just pray about it … nuff said.

CHAPTER 5

Overcoming Negative Emotions
When Life Happens to You

Life happens to us all no matter what the upbringing we have had as we live day-to-day by the grace of God; good things and bad things happen to us, and we have no control over them, except how we respond to them. Someone once said, "Life is 20 percent what happens to you and 80 percent of how you respond to it!" Our afflictions can make us very bitter about life, or it can become a springboard for our success! It all depends on how we position our attitude about what has happened to us or what is happening to us! Believe me, keeping an attitude that is optimistic in the face of your adversity is extremely difficult; it is not easy to do but is necessary for you to overcome and thrive again. It takes discipline to do this...heh, haa...

I'm still learning this truth, just like you, readers. As the old saying goes, "Altitude corresponds to our attitude." God allows things to happen to us, both good and bad, that we may know him better and grow spiritually. Affliction is for our good...heh, haa...even though it doesn't feel that way.

The Bible declares in 2 Corinthians chapter 4 verses 17-18.
"For our light, affliction, which is but for a moment, is working for us a far more exceeding and eternal weight of glory. While we do not look at the things which are seen, but at the things which are not seen. For the things which are seen are temporary, but the things which are not seen are eternal!" "Amen," I say to that statement. This is an encouraging promise from the Lord, via his apostle Paul, to the church at Corinth and the body of Christ at large.

$$*****$$

The way that I personally combat negative emotions when situations arise in my life is by using the word of God; I speak the scriptures over my situation by faith, over my mind by praying for myself.

I get into a posture of prayer and lay my hands on my own head as I recite 2 Corinthians chapter 10 verses 3-5, "For though we walk in the flesh, we do not war according to the flesh."

For the weapons of our warfare are not carnal, but mighty in God, for the pulling down of strongholds, casting down arguments and every high thing that exalts itself against the knowledge of God, bringing every thought into captivity to the obedience of Christ!' Reciting this scripture in prayer over your own mind by faith will remove the negative thoughts you may have and encourage you instead of discouraging you.

This is a scripture of spiritual warfare for your mind to obtain peace in the Lord Jesus Christ. Whenever I feel overwhelmed by negative thoughts and emotions (i.e., suicidal thoughts, fearfulness, anger, or depression where I'm ready to give up on life), then I pray this scripture over my mind and then I can feel better about my circumstances, without them changing one bit! Yeah, did you read what I just said? Your circumstance or situation don't have to change, one bit, before you can feel better emotionally. Believe that!

That was what the "01 Saints of God" a.k.a. believers in Christ declared back in the day, "I gotta run on, to see what the end is gonna be." Declarations like this helped them not to give up on life. So, it helps to press your way or endure hardship as a good soldier of Jesus Christ. The Bible also says in Galatians chapter 6 verse 9, "And let us not grow weary while doing good, for in due season, we shall reap, if we do not lose heart." You will reap victory, for you see, faith does not say everything will work out the way that you want it to regardless of how your situation works out; faith in God says he will work things out for your good! So, trust God and not your circumstance! Don't quit on God, keep believing in him! Nuff said...

CHAPTER 6

The Practice of Pressing Your Way through Trials and Circumstances

The practice of pressing your way through a difficult situation is more of a mind-set of "sticking to what you have begun and not quitting." I call this the press mind-set. I can think of various times in my life when things got not only difficult to deal with, but they became unbearable. In October 2015, I lost my job as an aircraft mechanic (I was released after only eight months of getting hired) all of a sudden.

I had no income, except for my wife's, and she didn't make enough to support the household on just her salary.

We had huge expenditures that were immediately due (i.e, mortgage payment, two car payments, car insurance, etc.). Despite all this financial pressure, I still had to negotiate payment arrangements with my various creditors while applying for work. My mindset during this season was to stay focused on God's word, which was my only source of encouragement, along with plenty of prayer time with the Lord for direction and decision-making. You must keep a level head when situations suddenly arise in your life. Keep your faith focused on what the Lord has said in his word (Bible) and that will keep your mind-set in a press or never-give-up mode.

You must resist the overwhelming urge to *panic* or overreact when an unexpected situation begins to arise. It is because it you can discipline yourself that way, you will have a better and a more effective response to what has arisen in your life. The most important thing is to apply your faith to what the *Lord Most High God* a.k.a. Jesus Christ has already declared in his word (Bible). In the book of Isaiah chapter 40 verses 27-31, it declares, "Why do you say, O Jacob and speak O Israel, My way is hidden from the Lord and my just claim is passed over by my God"? Have you not known? Have you not heard?

* * * * *

The everlasting God, the Lord, the creator of the ends of the earth, neither faints nor is weary; his understanding is unsearchable.

He gives power to the weak, and to those who have no might, he increases strength. Even the youths shall faint and be weary, and the young man shall utterly fall. But those who wait on the Lord shall renew their strength; they shall mount up with wings like eagle; they shall run and not be weary. They shall walk and not faint. The bottom line is, put all of your faith and hope in God because he has promised, as you have just read, to strengthen you in your time of despair! *"PRAISE BE TO GOD,"*!!

Believe me, people, what I'm saying is much easier said than done. But the reason why I can tell you to believe God, with all that you have, is because I'm in a situation right now that seems hopeless for me and my family financially! We are four months behind in our mortgage right now and one vehicle has been repossessed already, and after being unemployed for a few times (myself), I am trusting the Lord Jesus Christ that the current new job that I am working works out for me. But rather than glorify my problems, I would rather focus more on my God who is bigger than my problems. Ya know? Heh, haa...so yeah, while I encourage you to not give up.

I'm encouraging myself to press ahead as well... un huh...

CHAPTER 7

Faith without Works Is Dead

One thing that I've come to realize in my service to the Lord Jesus Christ is that he is moved to work on your and my behalf when we put our faith in him, but the faith that we put in him must be accompanied by some action. I mean, if the Lord has told you to do something, then just obey him and do it! The Bible declares in the book of James chapter 2 verses 17-18, "Thus also faith by itself, if it does not have works is dead. But someone will say, "You have faith, and I have works, show me your faith without your works and I will show you my faith by my works."
We can't expect the Lord to move on our behalf unless we obey him, ya know!

A life lived by faith in God alone will challenge you, and it will take you places that you have never been. It can be exciting, but you can also allow the enemy of faith, "doubt and fear," to creep into your heart and mind if you're not careful while you patiently wait on the Lord. The way that you get rid of doubt and fear is by focusing on what God has said in his word; this is why the Bible must be the final authority over your life because when you do, God will always keep his word! He cannot Lie or change his mind about us…heh, haa… so trust God!

The Bible declares in the book of Hebrews chapter 11 verse 6, "But without faith, it is impossible to please him (God) for he who comes to God, must believe that he is and that he is a rewarder of those, who diligently seek him." So as a disciple of Christ, a.k.a. a disciplined follower of Jesus Christ, we must place our faith in Christ by obeying what he has told us to do already in the scriptures. We walk out our faith by obeying God on a daily basis-this pleases God!

* * * * *

When we obey God, we then have *peace* with God because there is nothing more peaceful than knowing that down on the inside (deep), you are pleasing God by what you are doing; this will bring God glory in the end! I mean, after all, the very purpose of mankind is to bring glory to God in the Earth; this is why he created you and I. Real faith as described in Hebrew chapter 11 verses 24-25 says it this way, "By faith Moses, when he became of age, refused to be called the Son of Pharaoh's daughter, choosing rather to suffer affliction with the people of God, than to enjoy the passing pleasures of Sin."

As we see in *Moses's case*, faith will cost you something, but as I've declared in this chapter title, "Faith without works is dead." You can't call yourself a Christian or a believer in Christ if you don't step out in faith like Jesus did when he walked the earth. When we do step out in faith (on what God has spoken), then we will see God's provision and favor. Obeying the uncompromised word of God is paramount in the life of a believer in Christ. Once you decide in your heart to obey the Lord, in whatever you believe that he is calling you to do, then you must place your faith in what he has said. I am writing this book by faith as I believe that it will encourage someone along the way from my personal walk with God. So be encouraged, people because the Lord loves you and he has a dynamic plan for your life! Believe God despite what you're going through… nuff said!

Side note: Are you saved? Do you know Jesus Christ as personal friend? Acknowledge your sin, "for all have sinned and come short of the glory of God" (Rom. 3:23). Ask God (verbally) to forgive you of your sins repent or turn away from sin). "Repent ye therefore and be converted, that your sins may be blotted out' (Acts 3:19). Believe in Jesus Christ. "For God so loved the world, that he gave his only begotten Son, that whoever believeth in him, should not perish, but have everlasting life" (John 3:16). Make your decision. "If thou shalt confess with thy mouth the Lord Jesus and shalt believe in thine heart that God hath raised him from the dead, thou shalt be saved" (Rom. 10:9).

Will you pray to God something like this? God, I'm convinced I am a *sinner*, and that Christ alone can save me. I willingly repent for my sinful life and believe Jesus Christ died for me!

I want to receive him as my personal savior now! If you just prayed that prayer with your whole heart and really meant it, then please call this number to help you with your walk with Christ! Call 1-800-700-7000, there will be a prayer counselor standing by twenty-four hours to help you figure out how to walk out your relationship with Jesus Christ! Praise God and welcome to the kingdom of God!

God bless you!

Of Ash and Flames

Cam A. Roze

Published by Cam A. Roze, 2023.

This is a work of fiction. Similarities to real people, places, or events are entirely coincidental.

OF ASH AND FLAMES

First edition. January 16, 2023.

Copyright © 2023 Cam A. Roze.

Written by Cam A. Roze.

Of Ash and Flames

KAM A. POZE

Of Ashes and Flames

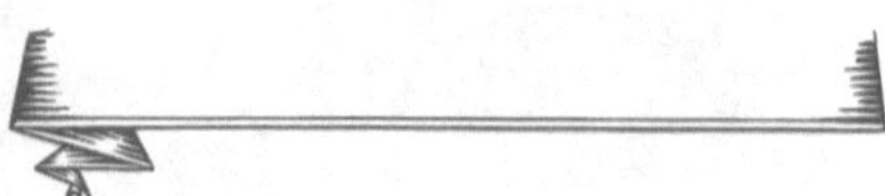

AGE RATING: ALL PUBLIC
Category: Short Story

A small fire genasi experiences life in a very unique way, the other half of her tries to take force, what will become of the Genasi?

Silicia, The Split And An Inferno of Torment

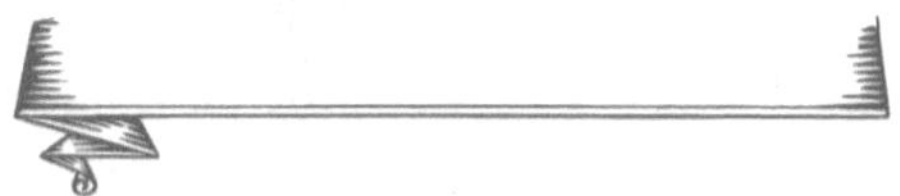

SILICIA, BORN OF TWO fine fire genasi, full of passion. From the elemental tribe of the Southhe tribe had its ways and its wages in wars throughout many of its time and historic teachings. Her father was a tribe warrior who had fought many wars against goblins, orcs, dragonborn and even kobolds.

The tribe had her mother known to be a handy armorer to the tribe, working metals into many sorts. She crafted armors and weapons. She even had made cooking wares of various sorts.

Silicia grew up humbly in this village. She had only begun to walk when the tribe had been invaded. Many speculate the actual events including the lone surviving child. Silicia only would remember the raid to burn the entirety of her home being burnt down to ashes. The screams would always haunt her, although whatever she had seen in that time had been blocked from memory.

Silicia, who'd wandered into the woods and was discovered by a group of elves, was only a small child at the time. The elves decided to try and raise her as one of their kind, seeing as the fire genasi at this time had seemed to vanish from the island.

The elves had taught her many amazing things, like many languages. Her one gift was the library when settled into Inaso, on the far southeast of the island. She knew something was wrong when she hit age five, realizing there were fragmented times happening. She tried to pretend these things were not to occur. Even so the screams from her past would haunt her mind.

The elves had placed her with the orphans. The elves referred to these as the lost ones. Silicia related heavily to the new label, she indeed was lost. Her father and mother to never be seen again. Her mind was fragmented, even beyond her feeling of it.

As the children of the orphanage she shared with them had quickly understood, was that the young girl couldn't handle being around too much water. They would begin to ostracize her for her racial alignment to fire. The genasi was a proud child. The child knew this was a threat to her being. She grew colder as time went forward.

Her head would be hurting constantly and not know why. the time gaps happened more and more often. The children continued to assault her with many insults. She felt darkness within her grow. She tried her best to endure everything she had gone through. At age eight she learned she only could handle so much, awakening the sorceress within her.

One fateful night a short drow of twenty years of age went in to take in a child. He felt the need to share his recent abundance due to his discovery of a map. The drow had deep purple eyes and he seemed to be hypnotic to the people around. She wanted the man to take her. She wanted to learn how to be anted by others, to learn to project a presence like his.

The man was repulsed by her presence in the room. He spat to her. She backed away startled, her hair turned blue from the emotional hurt. The elf panicked and kicked Silicia into the hallway before slamming the door. Her mind began to feel as if it were being sawn in half, only managing to kneel, holding her head. That was the night she can never remember, no matter how hard she would try in coming years. Everyone on the island knows what happened but her on that night. She started to giggle as her head hurt.

"I just wanna play..." Silicia would say muffled from the other side of the door. Her voice almost as deep as a demons.

"But, I like these ones." Silicia would reply in a high pitched whine. "Why do you want to hurt everything?"

"I want the world to be beautiful. Fire is pretty, so let's watch the world burn." Her deepened voice would reply to the higher pitched.

Both voices filled the air for miles. The orphanage was just starting to begin taking everyone outside as quickly as possible. The efforts only saved six individuals that day. Only the sound of the flames would be heard, drowning the sounds of screams that filled the orphanage. Only the walls would be seen, windows with sheer black flames coming out from them. Thick black smokes filled the skies. Silicia, the fire starter that left nothing but rubble and ash surrounding her. No bones were ever discovered so no proper burial ever occurred. She would be on her knees in the rubble.

Silicia would manage her way from her knees holding the right hand side of her face. The little girl walked from the rubble to only see the librarian of the area offer his hand. He seemed unafraid. She was giggling as she approached the elvish librarian. The librarian thought she must have been crying, as a survivor to the tragedy.

"—I'll watch you burn like pretty fire too." Her deeper voice spoke.

"Silicia-" He would try to answer.

"Call me Sil." She would reply as she walked away.

No one followed her. She eventually woke to her own self again, utterly lost and confused. Not able to recall the events, she would aim to find civilization again. She wandered into a deep forest.

She grew quickly being witty in the woods. Silicia, hitting the age of sixteen, had made her own way of surviving in the forest. She had learned of her magic ability as a sorceress and began to constantly push to evolve her knowledge. She had even learned to speak to certain animals. She knew if she had a place to learn and focus, she would be able to have grand ability. She craved that strength of ability. All knowledge was Silicia's goal.

One day, she was headed to the western side of the island, she encountered a strange young girl, who had covered herself in wolves pelts. Silicia had an interest in the seemingly defenseless child. The child, little to Silicia's knowledge, was actually older than herself. The wolf pelt covered one, had been on the run from her pack for some time.

Silicia and the were-being had become quite close as friends in the remaining time in the forest. They had a lot of fun in the woods, although the were-being was not aware. a few weeks had gone by before they even got to know one anothers names. the were-being was names Athii, as she had been raised in the woods by her old pack, where she was supposed to be the next in line for being the alpha female. Athii had no interest in such ideas.

Silicia and Athii relocated to the far west of the island. Silicia helped Athii build her home north to Ostros. Silicia wished Athii the best, hoping they would meet again one day.

Silicia decided she would go onward in life by adventuring for her means of living. She longed to belong somewhere, anywhere, so long as she would fit in. Somewhere people would like her. She went forth on her adventures to fulfill the longing within the void left in her heart. She went to Ostros, a city of giants, to discover the tieflings, a divine race as she came to understand.

She stayed with them for a while to learn the language of Infernal. She also went forward to study the language of the giants. She hoped to gain their trust and asked to settle with them, to only get rejected by the settlement. She took that as she was only being sent onward to complete more work.

She left the large settlement for a place named Boulders Gates, where the races were very mixed. No one hardly took notice of her appearance or race. It seemed everyone here had a place to belong. She was eager to see all this city had to offer. She had hoped that she finally found the place that she belonged.

She stayed in a tavern ran by an old fire Genasi, named Eladorn within the city walls. She had explained everything as she recalled it to the fire genasi, hoping for once that she would find someone who understood. He admittedly didn't relate. Even so, he hired her to be his barkeep. She liked this idea. During the time she worked with Eladorn, she had made the establishment stand out. Most of the time people would be disregarding the warm ales as they got in their service at the tavern.

Eladorn had taken notice, the young Gensai, Silicia had no idea how to fix this issue. No one wanted warm ale but, most were too polite to mention such a thing to Silicia. Eladorn himself being a sorcerer of sorts, took the time to teach Silicia a spell known as 'Ice Knife' which she had started to utilize to keep the ale fresh and cool. They had a ton of grand success in this endeavor, fixing the only issue the tavern had.

Silicia had learned how to prepare many foods with her natural elemental alignment. Eladorn took pride in teaching the younger fire genasi. He knew she had a lot of potential and power tucked away within. he could sense the darkness of her heart still present even with the time passed by. He trusted her, none the less.

Eladorn after five years of successfully teaching Silicia. On the day that they claimed her birthday to be, he gave her the deed to the tavern. The Dragons Tankard would be hers for as long as she had decided so. Eladorn explained he would be back again one day, however, it would not to be her aid, but to ask for it instead.

They spent the entire day celebrating with some of the locals. A small knit community was beginning to form, she was becoming a bit of an icon in the community. Everyone had a reason to adore Silicia, whether it was from service at the tavern, or simply understanding the other people in the community. She felt valued. She felt she belonged. Silicia earned her place in Boulders Gates. She went to bed early that night in a drunken bliss.

Eladorn disappeared that night, leaving Silicia to the tavern. The tavern ran smoothly for a week. She had everyone satisfied with her services, even to the point she had started to save enough gold for an addition to the tavern. She wanted to offer an inn for passersby. Surely this would be welcome to offer travelers a place to stay.

Then one fateful day, a young drow entered the tavern with a water genasi, claiming they were the heroes of this island.

The drow had a faintly memorable feature, deep purple eyes. Silicia knew better. Eladorn would have been a true hero in her mind. She could feel a pulse wash over her, to no effect on her.

"So, where's Eladorn?" The drow asked Silicia.

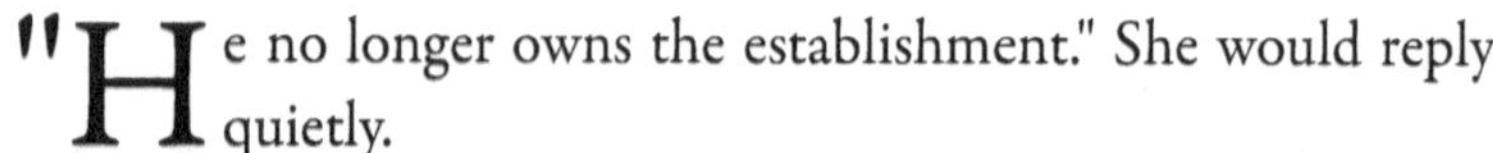

"He no longer owns the establishment." She would reply quietly.

"So then who owns it?" The drow asked her, the water genasi keeping a hand on the drows shoulder.

"I own this place now." Silicia said.

"Where did Eladorn go?" The drow spoke with haste. aggression was tense in his voice.

"He's resuming his adventuring." Silicia would say.

"You killed him didn't you? For the deed?" The drow spoke.

"Thats rude..." The water genasi interjeted.

"I.. did... no... such.. thing..." Silicia's breathing got heavy.

"Oh, push a button did I?" The drow would taunt.

"Fire..." Silicia mumbled as she gripped her head.

"Miss... are you okay?" The water genasi would try to check on Silicia.

Within the blink of an eye Silicia bursts into an inferno of black flames. Her eyes faded into jet black like coals. She grabbed the water genasi by the shirt and threw her through the front door, off the doors hinges The genasi ended up in the cobblestone streets, laying on their back, hardly breathing.

"You're gonna regret that, girl." The drow growled at Silicia. The tavern slowly emptied until it was just them in the dining area.

"No, I am gonna make you pretty like fire." Silicia said with a smile, the voice drop happening yet again. This time, she didn't even get a hint that she was losing herself.

The drow drew their blade. Just as quick as they drew it Silicia had her hands over the sword. She smiled at the drow, his panic beginning to set in. His eyes flashed a purple color into her eyes, besides just causing her to get irritated, it had not effect. The drow wore an expression of sheer disbelief.

She twisted her hands and snapped the heated blade from her touch. Never had the drow experienced such terror. She laid a hand on the drow's cheek, kissing him gently, as he tried to scream from the burning she ensued on his body. She let her kiss go, the drows body dropped to the floor. Smoke raised from the seared body of the drow. Silicia believed the drow to be dead.

Silicia dragged out the body into the street for the water genasi to dispose of. She smiled to the water genasi. The water genasi was frozen in terror. She ran off to hide, not to be heard of for many years to come. The water genasi will never forget the events she encountered with Silicia that fateful day.

Silicia's reputation as twin spirited was rampid and spreading all over the island. Many would travel to her tavern for business. Many would request to be her apprentice in many of her crafts. She was a wise genasi, however, there was a part of Silicia everyone knew to get away from.

The locals help Silicia on a regular basis now, her being a vital cornerstone to the community. They all have come to adore her. When she splits now, they help her rebuild the tragic losses. They know she always means the best. Most have learned now just what to avoid talking about near her.

Silicia, from ash and flame, traveled through hells beyond the typical. She gained her respect by becoming a barmaid. Then a proprietor, none the less.Who ever would have thought a bar was the best place for a fire genasi.

Don't miss out!

Visit the website below and you can sign up to receive emails whenever Cam A. Roze publishes a new book. There's no charge and no obligation.

https://books2read.com/r/B-A-CUFV-CAPEC

BOOKS 2 READ

Connecting independent readers to independent writers.

About the Author

Cam A. Roze is a Dark Fantasy Author. they strive to have immersive worlds and rich lore in all of their endeavors